SKIN

BODYWORKS

Tracy Maurer

The Rourke Corporation, Inc.
Vero Beach, Florida 32964

Tracy M. Maurer specializes in non-fiction and business writing. Her most recently published children's books include the Let's Dance Series, also from Rourke Publishing.

With appreciation to Lois M. Nelson, Mac and Lynn Mitchell, Paige Henson, Dr. Victoria Brown - Georgia College and State University, and Sharon Vacula.

PHOTO CREDITS:
© Timothy L. Vacula: cover, pages 4, 13, 15, 17,; © Lois M. Nelson: title page, pages 12, 15, 21; © Diane Farleo: page 18; courtesy of Dr. Victoria Brown - Georgia College and State University: page 10

ILLUSTRATION: © Todd Tennyson: page 8

EDITORIAL SERVICES: Janice L. Smith for Penworthy Learning Systems

CREATIVE SERVICES: East Coast Studios, Merritt Island, Florida

Library of Congress Cataloging-in-Publication Data

Maurer, Tracy, 1965-
   Skin / by Tracy Maurer.
     p. cm. — (Bodyworks)
   Summary: Describes the qualities and parts of our skin and how it functions as a protective covering and a warning system for our bodies.
   ISBN 0-86593-582-3
   1. Skin Juvenile literature. [1. Skin.] I. Title. II. Series: Maurer, Tracy, 1965- Bodyworks.
QP88.4.M38 1999
612.7'9—dc21
                                      99-23374
                                           CIP

Printed in the USA

TABLE OF CONTENTS

THE BODY'S LARGEST ORGAN

The next time you take a bath, think about your skin. About two and a half yards of skin covers your bones. Skin is your body's largest organ.

The thickness of your skin changes all over your body. Your eyelids have thin skin. Your hands and feet have very thick skin.

None of your skin looks smooth up close. Look at your fingertips. The curly lines there make your fingerprint. No one else has fingerprints the same as yours!

Skin keeps your insides safe from the outside world. Sunscreen protects your skin from the sun.

THE OUTER SKIN

Like an onion, skin has many layers. Deep holes dot the outer layer, or the **epidermis** (EP i DER miss). One hair grows out of each hole. Millions of hairs cover your body. About 100,000 hairs top your head. Each hair there grows nonstop for two to six years. Then it falls out to make room for a new one.

Hair and fingernails grow from live **cells** (SELZ) deep down in the skin. The parts you see are dead cells mixed with a tough **protein** (PRO teen). That's why cutting your hair or fingernails doesn't hurt.

Brushing helps pull out the hair you lose every day.

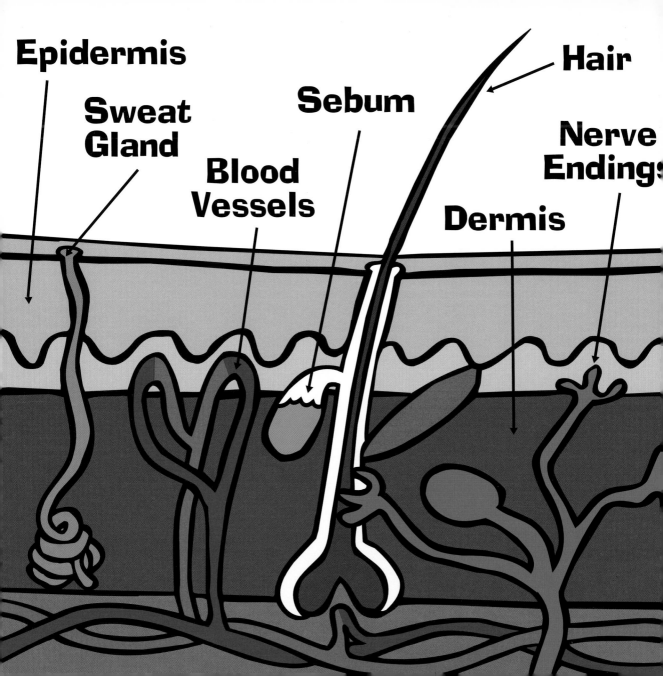

LAYERS BELOW

New cells push up from lower skin layers. Dead skin cells fall off the epidermis like flakes of old paint. About a million cells fall off every 40 minutes.

The **dermis** (DER miss), or inner skin, forms a layer under the epidermis. This layer holds sweat glands, **blood vessels** (BLUD VESS ulz), nerves, and hair roots. Fatty tissue pads the dermis. It protects inside parts and helps keep the body warm.

The skin has two layers, called dermis and epidermis.

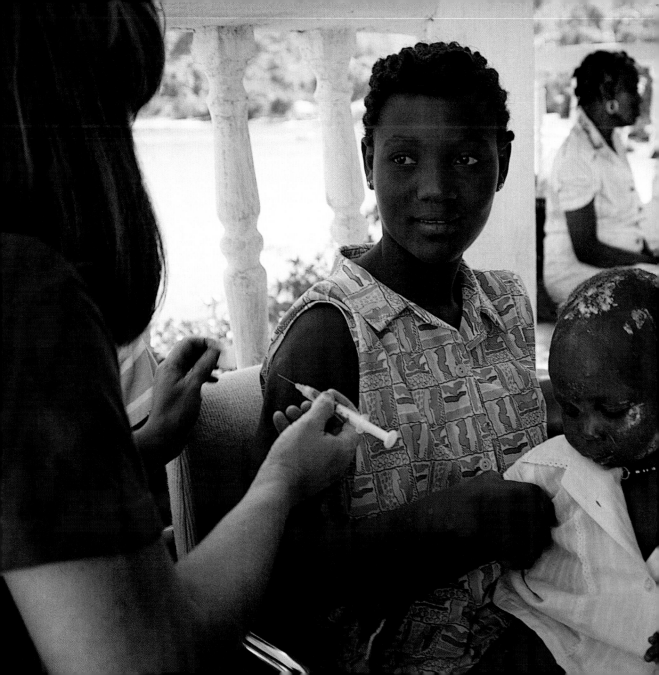

THE WARNING SYSTEM

Nerves flow throughout the dermis. More nerves exist on body parts that touch the outside world often. For example, your fingertips have many nerves. Some **nerve endings** (NERV END ingz) sense heat or cold. Others sense pressure or pain. The amount of pain you feel depends on how many nerve endings are affected. Sticking your finger with a pin hits fewer nerve endings and causes less pain than stepping on a nail.

Nerve endings send signals to your brain. This helps protect you from hurting yourself too badly.

Nerve endings warn the
brain of pain.

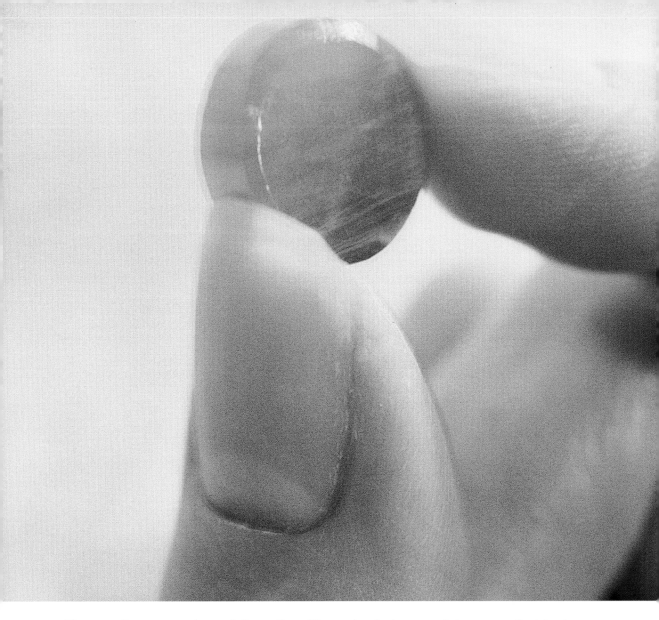

Fingernails protect the soft fingertips. They also help you pick up small objects. Cells in fingernails are dead.

Patches of melanin form freckles.

SKIN COLORS

Melanin (MEL uh nin) gives skin its color. Cells in the body make melanin. Everyone has about the same number of these cells. The amount of melanin made by the cells is different for each person. The more melanin in a person's skin, the darker its color. Some people can't make melanin. They have no color, not even in their eyes. This is called **albinism** (AL buh NIZ um).

Melanin protects skin from the sun's harmful rays. Extra melanin floods your skin's cells to shade them from bright sunlight. Then you "tan."

Melanin gives your skin its color.

A SHIELD

Skin is your body's waterproof shield against germs, or **bacteria** (bak TEER ee uh). Many bad bacteria fall off the top layer along with the dead cells. Others die in the salty sweat and oily **sebum** (SEE bum) that rise from lower layers. Sebum gives your hair and skin wetness to keep them from cracking.

Even freshly cleaned skin may have harmless germs. Some of these germs also fight off bad bacteria.

Lotion adds wetness when skin dries out.

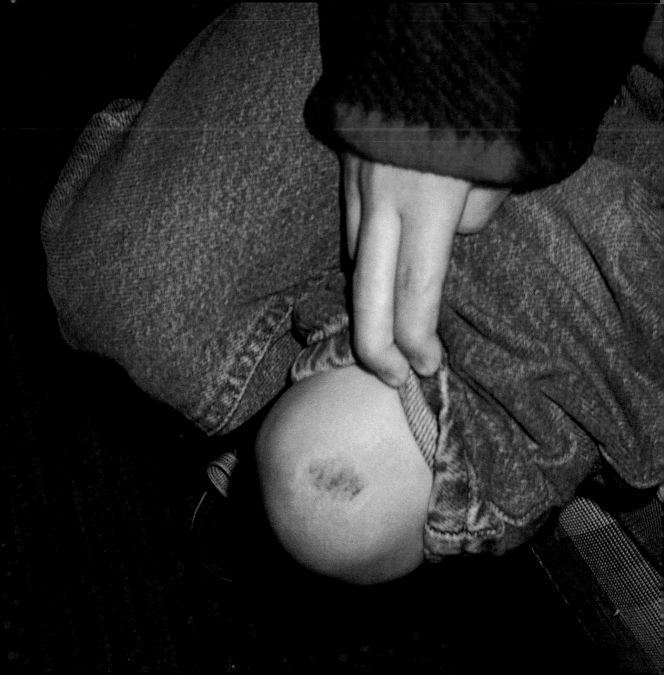

ITCHY SKIN

You scratch an itch to stop it. What starts it? Itches often start when dry air or sweat bothers the skin. Illnesses such as chicken pox can make skin itch. An **allergy** (AL er jee) to anything may create itches. Even being worried can cause itches.

Skin gives clues about your health. Skin may redden with a fever. It can look blue if you are too cold. Skin shows how you feel, too. Your cheeks might turn pink if you feel shy. Skin may become pale if you feel afraid or angry.

Skin can fix itself. New cells move to the top layer every day. Sometimes the skin itches as it heals.

SWEAT AND GOOSE BUMPS

Skin helps keep your body warm—at about 98.6°F (37°C). When you feel too hot, sweat flows from the sweat glands in the dermis. Water in the sweat cools your skin as it dries. It leaves salt and odor behind. Also, blood vessels widen so that more blood pumps through your skin. The heat that escapes helps to cool the body.

To warm you, blood vessels narrow and slow the blood flow. You shiver when certain muscles tighten. Shivering helps to warm your body. Other muscles pull up the hairs on your body. They make goose bumps.

Skin works to keep your body temperature the same in all kinds of weather.

THE GREAT HEALER

Have you ever cut your knee? It bled for a bit, then stopped. Maybe a scab grew over the knee. Soon it looked as good as new! Skin fixes itself. Scratches, cuts, sunburns—the skin will heal them all. Cells move from the bottom of the epidermis to the top. The trip takes four to five weeks.

Skin cannot fix some sun damage. Put on sunscreen lotion when you play in the sun. Take care of your skin so that it can take care of you.

GLOSSARY

albinism (AL buh NIZ um) — the lack of color in the skin's cells

allergy (AL er jee) — sneezing, itching, watery eyes or other bad reaction to pets, plants, foods or anything else

bacteria (bak TEER ee uh) — tiny living things that are sometimes good for the body and sometimes make the body sick

blood vessels (BLUD VESS ulz) — tubes called arteries and veins that move the blood through the body

cells (SELZ) — the tiny building blocks that make up all people, animals, and plants

dermis (DER miss) — the layer under the top layer of skin, also called the inner skin

epidermis (EP i DER miss) — the outer most layer of skin

melanin (MEL uh nin) — the brown color in the cells of the skin, hair, and other body parts

nerve endings (NERV END ingz) — the parts of the signal fibers closest to the skin's surface

protein (PRO teen) — a natural building block made by the body

sebum (SEE bum) — oil that protects the skin and hair

INDEX

FURTHER READING:

Find out more about Bodyworks with these helpful books:

• Walker, Richard. *The Children's Atlas of the Human Body.* Brookfield, Connecticut: The Millbrook Press, 1994.

• Miller, Jonathan, and David Pelham. *The Human Body: The Classic Three-Dimensional Book.* New York: Penguin Books, 1983.

• Williams, Dr. Frances. *Inside Guides: Human Body.* New York: DK Publishing, 1997.

On CD-ROM

• *The Family Doctor,* 3rd Edition. Edited by Allan H. Bruckheim, M.D. © Creative Multimedia, 1993-1994.

SAINT MARY'S SCHOOL
309 E. Chestnut Street
Lancaster, Ohio 43130